Vulnerable Evangelism

The Way of Jesus

John Holmes

Canon Missioner, Diocese of Wakefield
Member of the College of Evangelists

GROVE BOOKS LIMITED

RIDLEY HALL RD CAMBRIDGE CB3 9HU

Contents

The Cover Illustration is by Peter Ashton, from an idea by Steve Simpson

First Impression May 2001
Reprinted with revisions November 2003
ISSN 1367-0840
ISBN 1 85174 464 9

Beyond the Caricature

The evangelist nearly always gets a bad press. In the media he (it usually is a he) is depicted as loud and insensitive, overintense, humourless and manipulative—it is the image of the pushy salesman.[1]

It was a Saturday morning in 1999. I was in a market town in the Fens, attending a friend's wedding. My wife and I had an hour or two to spare to look around. The central square of the town was busy—market stalls, charities displaying their goods, and crowded shops. Yet as I looked across the square I noticed one part of it was empty. Then I saw why. A man was speaking in a loud voice, apparently to no-one in particular. As I got nearer to him I realized he was an evangelist seeking to commend the Christian faith to his hearers. But his loud voice, brash tone, and Bible waved accusingly had the effect of ensuring people gave him a wide berth, hurrying past with their heads down. As John Drane has said, 'We have too many evangelists like Rambo and too few like Jesus Christ.' The caricature lives.

Yet as I looked across the square I noticed one part of it was empty. Then I saw why.

Of course most evangelists are not like that. As the members of the Working Party who produced the *Good News People* Report concluded:

As we met evangelists round the country, we realized that the caricature was very different from these humble men and women of God who simply had a desire to communicate a faith that had come to mean so much to them, and who longed to see others enter into a relationship with God.[2]

From the day I first responded to Jesus I have sought to share the love of God with others. That has been the fundamental motivation behind my ministry as a parish priest and, in recent years, as a diocesan missioner. I have never had a problem with the word 'evangelism' nor the task to which that word refers—sharing the good news of God's love for the whole creation in Jesus Christ. But I have often reflected on how to fulfil that task in a way that is appropriate to the person or the community with whom I am engaged and which is true to Jesus.

Here is the challenge that lies behind the writing of this booklet. For, unlike me, some Christians do have a problem with the word 'evangelism' and often this is linked with a caricature of the evangelist whose style is a long way from that of Jesus.

As diocesan missioner, I was getting ready to speak at a deanery chapter when the rural dean, a friend of mine, leaned over to me and said in my ear, 'Don't mention the E-word here!' Evangelism had been a real bone of contention in that deanery and a particular model of evangelism enthusiastically advocated by some had effectively alienated others. Clearly I was in a minefield and I had to proceed with caution.

A few weeks before, I had been at a PCC meeting specifically to speak about evangelism. As part of the presentation I had shown various statements about mission and evangelism which I felt could be helpful. One was the remark of St Francis of Assisi, 'Go into the world and proclaim the gospel. Use words if you have to.' To encourage engagement with St Francis' message I covered up 'words' in the quotation.

> GO INTO THE WORLD AND PROCLAIM THE GOSPEL.
>
> USE _____ IF YOU HAVE TO.

I asked if anyone could guess what the missing word was. There was a deep silence. Then one of the churchwardens attempted an answer. 'Is it "force"?'

> GO INTO THE WORLD AND PROCLAIM THE GOSPEL.
>
> USE FORCE IF YOU HAVE TO.

As I recount that incident, people usually laugh heartily. At the time I was more saddened than amused. The answer of the mature and able Christian seemed to betray a profound caricature of evangelism which has been a stumbling block to many—within and outside the church. The most notable example in church history of 'evangelism' by force is the Crusades, and they have stained Christian relations with Muslim and Jew ever since. We have to repent of what has sometimes been undertaken by our brothers and sisters in the name of Christ and seek a better way. Jesus provides us with that way.

It is the life and death of Jesus that provide the best starting point for the nature and work of the evangelist. We see in the ministry of Jesus and in the way he engaged with people, in his suffering and

It is the life and death of Jesus that provide the best starting point for the nature and work of the evangelist

death on the cross as our wounded healer and in the ministry of disciples sent out as 'lambs among wolves' (Luke 10.3) a way of evangelism beyond the caricature. It is a way that can be seen in today's church too—though those who practise it are often unaware of doing so. It is a way that can be best described as vulnerable evangelism. It is, I believe, a way that rings most true in our postmodern, post-Christendom society.

Questions for Reflection

- How do you understand 'evangelism' and 'evangelist'?
- How did you come to know the truth of the gospel for yourself?
- What incident(s)/story(s) from the gospels have most affected your faith story?

2   A Defining Moment

> I shall therefore prefer to find my joy and pride in the very things that are my weakness; and then the power of Christ will come and rest upon me. Hence I am well content, for Christ's sake, with weakness, contempt, persecution, hardship and frustration, for when I am weak, then I am strong.   (2 Corinthians 12.9–10 NEB)

Daniel lived with us for only five months but he has had an enormous influence on our lives. Daniel is another contemporary example of a consistent biblical theme—how God can use those who humanly speaking are small and insignificant to fulfil his purposes. I am confident he fulfils them still.

Daniel was born on 4th December 1975, our fourth child, a brother for Marianne, Patrick and Thomas. His short and happy life with us came to a sudden end on 4th May 1976 when he died in his cot. 'Sudden Infant Death Syndrome' the death certificate eventually declared. His death was an enormous shock to us and many people. Just before Christmas in 1975 Daniel had been baptized at a memorable service in the inner-city church where I was vicar. The two churchwardens were his godparents. A good friend from the Community of the Resurrection had preached and spoken of the birth of Daniel as a sign of hope. Then, just a few months later, Daniel had died. Had hope died with him? 'Where is God?' many asked.

Looking back at Daniel's death, it is clear we were reminded of certain lessons. First, the value of belonging to the church, the body of Christ—with all the support, prayer and love that we received. In a recent national survey in the USA, when people were asked, 'If you're in trouble, who could you turn to?' 86% said they would go to a member of a church congregation. No doubt a much smaller percentage would answer like that here, where church attendance is smaller. But the reality is the same for all those who know the value of belonging. 'We are the body of Christ' can roll off the tongue rather glibly in our worship, but to know something of the meaning of that in practice is a privilege.

The importance of honest prayer was a vital lesson too. To bring our hurt, confusion and questions to God as well as the joys and thanksgivings was fundamental to the spiritual growth we seemed to experience in the months that followed Daniel's death. Robert Warren recently said

> In the early days my faith was a celebration of 'Now I know the answers.' Now it is the faith that gives me the ability to live with the unanswered questions.[3]

Learning to live with the unanswered questions grew out of honest prayer and a new intimacy with God.

The healing power of the Eucharist to communicate God's presence and his reconciling work at the heart of our relationships and in the depth of our being was another significant lesson too we learnt afresh. As Richard Giles has said, 'The great thing about a sacrament is that God always turns up.'[4] The objective nature of God's sacramental presence in the Eucharist became a stronger reality.

earning to live with the unanswered questions grew out of honest prayer

We learnt another lesson too, the full significance of which has only dawned on me recently. It is a lesson about sharing the gospel in weakness—the lesson of vulnerable evangelism. I can best illustrate what I mean by that word by describing what happened one particular evening. The suddenness of Daniel's death meant the involvement of the coroner—as is usual for cot death—and the inevitable delay in arranging the funeral. So we decided to hold a Memorial Service for Daniel, a special Eucharist at the church to give thanks for Daniel and commend him to God. We arranged it for an evening so that as many could come as possible. And people did. The church was crowded—family and friends, some from a long way away, the church congregation and many others from the local community whom I could not recall ever having seen in church before. We had been involved in a vigorous campaign for the replacement of a local primary school, which our other children attended. Other campaigners came with everyone else to offer their support—and share our suffering.

The objective nature of God's sacramental presence in the Eucharist became a stronger reality

Though the service was led by friends, I spoke at the beginning and gave the address. I encouraged people to be honest with God and not to be afraid to weep. I said I believed we could see Jesus in this service—but not if we tried to deny our feelings. As the worship began, I am not sure which was louder, the singing or the sobbing. During the Eucharist we were aware of Jesus' presence with us strongly. He ministered to our broken hearts, he renewed our faith and confidence in him and he enabled us in our sorrow to sing out our love and trust in him. As the service finished, one of the older members of the congregation said to her husband, 'God *is* with us, isn't he?'

Through it all the gospel was proclaimed. In our sorrow and weakness, we spoke of the life and hope and strength that Jesus gives. Some who came that evening heard the gospel more clearly and authentically presented to them than ever before in their lives. From within our vulnerability as a family, as a community, the good news of Jesus, suffering, crucified and risen, was filling them with new healing life and reaching out to others. The repercussions were considerable.

When I look back over the life of that inner-city church and community—during the thirteen-and-a-half years we were there, I see how we sought more and more to be an evangelizing community. Still today that is true! During my time there we worked with many to share the love of God in Jesus Christ. Religious communities, the Church Army and noted evangelists like David Watson[5] and Billy Graham[6] all helped us in one way or another. By the time we left, the church had developed an ongoing programme of mission outreach expressed through a strong social commitment to the needs of the local community and regular evangelistic services and events within and beyond the church walls. Without doubt, though, the unexpected evangelistic impact of the memorial service for Daniel was as significant as any of the more organized and planned occasions following. We stumbled on what Paul had known earlier—the power of vulnerable evangelism.

> When I came to you brothers and sisters, I did not come proclaiming the mystery of God to you in lofty words or wisdom. For I decided to know nothing among you except Jesus Christ and him crucified. And I came to you in weakness and in fear and in much trembling.
>
> (1 Corinthians 2.1–3)

Questions for Reflection

- What lessons from the story of baby Daniel most connect with your experience?

- Have you shared the gospel in weakness? What effect did that have on others—and on yourself?

- What defining moment (or moments) have shaped your own call to share the gospel?

The Greatest Evangelist

3

> The other gods were strong, but thou wast weak;
> They rode, but thou didst stumble to a throne;
> But to our wounds only God's wounds can speak,
> And not a god has wounds, but thou alone.[7]

On a recent visit to the USA I noticed young people wearing wrist bands with the letters 'WWJD': 'What Would Jesus Do?' The same question appeared on several cars too—and has now come across the Atlantic. Asking the question does not always produce a straightforward answer. There are occasions in the New Testament when Jesus refused to get involved in people's disputes, as when he is asked to arbitrate between two brothers: 'Friend, who set me to be a judge or arbitrator over you?' (Luke 12.14). At times we can strain to get answers from the New Testament to questions that would not have been posed in that way.

Yet when we consider the task of evangelism, the work of sharing the love of God with others, it is surely appropriate that we begin with Jesus himself. We need to examine not just what he sought to share, but the way he shared it.

> A few years ago [says John Drane], I read through all the New Testament Gospels trying to identify Jesus' style of evangelization, hoping to find some guidelines that could be useful today. I was surprised that none of his messages could with certainty be identified with the sort of monologues that dominate much modern worship…Jesus' weakness and vulnerability is striking, and evangelists who wish to be as successful as he was should take a leaf from his book. We have something to share with others not because we are different, still less because we are experts and know it all, but because we are no different. We struggle with the same things as everyone else. We share the same tensions of joy and anger, success and failure, expectancy and frustration. But however threatening the chaos might be, we also meet God in it all—and that is really good news (for us as well as for others).[8]

I set out on my own journey of discovery, and like John Drane was struck at how Jesus' way of sharing the good news seemed a very long way from the pushy salesman caricature. As I re-read Matthew, Mark, Luke and John I noticed certain characteristics of Jesus' ministry that seemed vital to understanding how to share the gospel in today's world.

Jesus' Evangelistic Style

1. Person-Centred
Although the crowds listened to him gladly (Mark 12.37) Jesus' concern is usually for individuals. In Luke 5.1–11 Jesus responds to the desire of the crowds to hear the word of God. But the focus soon changes to Jesus' relationship with Peter. As the fishing boat is pushed out from the shore and the large catch made, Peter confesses his sense of unworthiness. But Jesus is encouraging. 'From now on you will be catching people.' Peter leaves everything and follows Jesus. Similarly when Jesus is walking through the crowds to the home of Jairus, the focus shifts from the crowd to an individual. 'Who touched me?' Jesus asks. Peter is amused at the question: 'Master, the crowds surround you and press in on you.' Jesus' concern, though, is unswervingly for the person in need, and as she acknowledges herself, he is able to speak kindly and reassuringly to her. 'Daughter, your faith has made you well. Go in peace' (Luke 8.42b–45).

The crowds are out, but Jesus' focus is on an individual

The day Jesus arrives at Jericho, the crowds are out too! But as before, Jesus' focus is on an individual, Zacchaeus, to whose house he invites himself, much to the consternation of the crowd. The change brought about in Zacchaeus' life—'Today salvation has come to this house'—is the fruit of Jesus' affirming and transforming love, personally given (Luke 19.1–10). There are many invalids at the Pool of Bethesda, but Jesus focused his concern on one in particular (John 5.2–9). As St Augustine has said, 'God loves every one of us, as if there was only one of us to love.' Jesus' ministry has that personal quality.

2. Listening First
As so often Jesus' ministry focuses on individuals, rather then crowds, it is not surprising to see that it usually begins in listening too. Henri Nouwen has said that Jesus is 'all ear.'

Jesus' first concern is to discover the person's need or longing, and frequently he does that by asking a question. Blind Bartimaeus' cry for mercy is heard by Jesus, who asks him, 'What do you want me to do for you?' His sight restored, Bartimaeus is liberated to follow Jesus and be a servant of others (Mark 10.46–52).

The two disciples on the road to Emmaus on Easter Day were reflecting on their sense of despair at what had happened in Jerusalem. Jesus draws this from them as he comes alongside them unrecognized and asks, 'What are you discussing with each other as you walk along?' (Luke 24.11). How can we speak the word of God, unless we first listen with the ears of Christ?

3. Not Intrusive
As Jesus reaches Emmaus with the two disciples he walks ahead 'as if he were going on.' They need to urge him strongly to stay. Jesus does not force his presence on people, or his message (Luke 24.28–29). The same characteristic is shown in Jesus'

His ministry is personal, appropriate and un-embarrassing

ministry to the blind man at Bethsaida where Jesus takes him by the hand and leads him out of the village. His ministry is personal, appropriate and un-embarrassing. He respects his individuality (Mark 8.22–23).

The famous Holman Hunt painting of the Light of the World—seen again by many in the millennium *Seeing Salvation* exhibition—makes the same point by leaving the initiative to open the door to the person inside, not to Christ. 'Listen! I am standing at the door, knocking; if you hear my voice and open the door, I will come in…' (Revelation 3.20).

4. Hospitable
Jesus is responsive to people however they come to him. The Pharisee Nicodemus comes by night, cautiously; he engages in a searching dialogue with Jesus (John 3.1ff). The father of the sick son comes desperately and implores Jesus' help when his disciples were unable to heal him (Luke 9.38–43). The woman in the crowd with internal bleeding comes secretly (Luke 8.42–44). The leper comes tentatively (Mark 1.40).

Jesus' word and touch and love bring life and wholeness and freedom to many who seek him. His hospitality is generous. 'Anyone who comes to me I will never drive away' (John 6.37).

5. Not Simplistic
'Jesus is the answer. What's the question?' This bumper-sticker approach to evangelism does a disservice to Jesus' own approach to people. With the Samaritan woman by Jacob's well, St John portrays Jesus as engaging in a long and perceptive dialogue ranging over issues of theology and the nature of worship as well as personal life. The woman's response to her fellow Samaritans—'Come and see a man who told me everything I have ever done!' illustrates the depth of the encounter. Significantly, Jesus stays two further days with the Samaritans at their invitation and 'many more believed' (John 4.6–42).

6. Compassionate

St Matthew is clear that compassion is at the heart of Jesus' ministry. 'When he saw the crowds he had compassion for them, because they were harassed and helpless, like sheep without a shepherd' (Matthew 9.36). Literally this means pain went through his guts. As Jurgen Moltman has said,

> He could not get the existence and situation of the people out of his mind, nor could he restrain the people from pressing around him. Their suffering came to him, went into him, so that he had to—and wanted to—identify with them.[9]

Jesus' compassion makes him profoundly vulnerable. He engages with people and gives himself to them at a deep level. As he seeks to share the Father's generous love there is a real cost.

7. Goes On Loving

Jesus goes on loving, even when there is no response. In St Mark's account of Jesus' encounter with the rich young ruler he says 'Jesus looking at him, loved him' (Mark 10.21). The look is in the same spirit of generous self-giving as that given to Peter when he had just denied him (Luke 22.51). John Finney defined an equation: 'Evangelism = Love.' Though doctrinally inadequate as he admits, it conveys the essential heart of the gospel and the way it should be shared. Jesus' ministry is an embodiment of that.

8. Rooted in his Relationship with his Father

The openness of Jesus' ministry could only have been sustained by his relationship with his Father. I mention this last, but it really belongs first, for it is his prior focus on his Father and on his Father's will that gives shape to all he does.

After an evening in Capernaum when Jesus had been actively ministering to the sick and troubled, Mark tells us: 'In the morning while it was still very dark, he got up and went out to a deserted place and there he prayed' (Mark 1.35). The time in prayer with his Father was crucial for what followed. When Simon and his companions found him—Luke speaks of 'crowds' looking for him (Luke 4.42)—Jesus is clear that he must move on to the neighbouring towns 'so that I may proclaim the message there also; for that is what I came out to do' (Mark 1.38). Throughout his ministry Jesus is seeking to fulfil his Father's purposes. 'My food is to do the will of him who sent me and complete his work' (John 4.34).

The characteristics of Jesus' ministry which reflect what I have called his 'evangelistic style' gives only half the picture. The vulnerability of Jesus is reflected not just in the way he related to people and his Father during the years of his ministry, but supremely in his suffering and death.[10] Pope Paul VI saw that clearly in his encyclical *Evangelization in the Modern World.*

> Jesus himself, the Good News of God, was the very first and greatest evangel-izer: he was so through and through: to perfection and to the point of the sacrifice of his earthly life.[11]

Jesus' Suffering and Death

No account of Jesus' way of sharing the love of God can be complete without a final focus on his suffering and death on the cross. Here his vulnerability is most fully revealed. Here his self-giving love takes passionate shape. Here he is the wounded healer, giving his life in obedience to his Father to be the means of liberation and healing for others. Russ Parker has said:

> At Calvary God demonstrated most painfully and in the greatest weakness, his abiding presence in times of overcoming and times of suffering. Both triumph and torture are brought to balance at this place where God chooses to be weak for our salvation.[12]

St Paul spoke of his weakness and fear and trembling when first speaking to the Corinthians about the mystery of God. He decided to know nothing among them except Jesus on the cross. In doing so he chose both the content and the method of vulnerable evangelism.

A True Story

'Is there anyone you specially want me to look out for?' the hospital chaplain was asking the ward sister, before he began his weekly visiting round. 'Yes there is,' she answered. 'The woman in the end bed. She's very bitter, especially against God. I doubt whether she will allow you to speak to her.'

The chaplain followed his usual practice of speaking to all the patients on the ward. People were pleased to spend a few moments with him or have a longer chat when it seemed necessary. As he approached the end bed, though, the woman turned away from him. 'Don't come near me! Don't talk to me!' she barked. 'God's got me in a trap!' The chaplain attempted to respond but the woman was adamant. 'God's got me in a trap!'

The following week, the chaplain bought a small crucifix, just the right size to hold in your hand, and took it with him to the ward. The woman was still there in the end bed. She was a little weaker than before, but she still called out to the chaplain as he approached. 'Don't come near me! God's got me in a trap!' This time he did not try to argue. He just moved forward quickly, put

13

The suffering and vulnerable Christ brought wholeness and peace

the crucifix into the woman's hand and said, 'God's in the trap with you.' Then he left.

When he visited the ward next week, the sister was looking out for him. 'Something remarkable has happened in the ward this week,' she told him eagerly. 'The woman in the end bed. She died three days ago. She had been very poorly. But what was remarkable was this. She died not bitter, but serene. Somehow all the bitterness seemed to drain away from her. And she never let go of that crucifix.'

The wounded healer was with her to heal. The suffering and vulnerable Christ brought wholeness and peace and the only word spoken was: 'God's in the trap with you.'

Questions for Reflection

- Looking at the characteristics of Jesus' evangelistic style, what are the implications for our own way of sharing the gospel?
- What other characteristics of Jesus' ministry are important for us too?
- What does the suffering and death of Jesus mean for our own journey of faith and evangelistic ministry?

The Evangelizing Community 4

> My friends, think what sort of people you are, whom God has called. Few of you are wise by any human standard, few powerful or of noble birth. Yet to shame the wise, God has chosen what the world counts folly and to shame what is strong, God has chosen what the world counts weakness. He has chosen things without rank or standing in the world, mere nothings, to overthrow the existing order. So no place is left for any human pride in the presence of God. By God's act you are in Christ Jesus: God has made him our wisdom, and in him we have our righteousness, our holiness, our liberation. Therefore in the words of Scripture, 'If anyone must boast, let him boast of the Lord.'
>
> (1 Corinthians 1.26–31 REB)

How can a Christian community seek to share the gospel today? I began to find an answer some years ago when I was appointed to an inner-city parish in south Leeds.

Every year the church celebrated its patronal festival on 18th October, St Luke's Day, so year after year I found myself preaching on the gospel appointed for that day, Luke 10.1–9. Over the years we were there—and in the years since— this passage has shed more and more light on the evangelizing task we were called to and the way it could be fulfilled. Working as a diocesan missioner, I have seen how the principles implicit in this passage resonate particularly with the task we face in contemporary Britain.

A Biblical Paradigm

The Seventy
'After this the Lord appointed seventy others.' (Luke 10.1) Only in Luke's gospel do we find Jesus sending out a large band of disciples. Some have argued therefore that this passage is simply a variant of Matthew's account of the sending out of the twelve. But that seems unlikely, as Luke has just recorded the mission of the twelve. Relating them so closely to one another suggests that he viewed them as distinct.

The seventy are likely, then, to refer to other followers of Jesus than the twelve. For the Jews seventy was a symbolic number. There were seventy elders who were chosen to help Moses with the task of leading and directing the people in the wilderness. Seventy was also the number of the Sanhedrin, the supreme council of the Jews. Seventy was held to be symbolic of the nations of the world[13]—a reminder that the gospel is for the whole world. John Moorman commented that 'We do not know how many people were travelling with him towards Jerusalem; but the seventy must have represented a large proportion of the party.'[14] Whatever the truth of these conjectures, Jesus sent the disciples ahead of him in pairs.

A Vulnerable Mission

Jesus sends the seventy out in pairs, 'like lambs into the midst of wolves' (Luke 10.3). The vulnerable evangelist commits his followers to the way of vulnerability. Colin Morris has said, 'The gospel cannot be proclaimed by the strong to the weak, but only by the weak to the strong.'[15] The vulnerability of the seventy consists of two things: first the opposition and indifference they will face; and secondly their small numbers in the face of a large task. They go then not in their own strength, but in reliance upon God. This reliance is the first aspect of the mission they—and we—undertake.

Prayer

'The harvest is plentiful, but the labourers are few: therefore ask the Lord of the harvest to send out labourers into his harvest' (Luke 10.2). There is much work to do, but first Jesus bids his followers look to the Lord of the harvest. Henri Nouwen has said:

> Prayer requires that we stand in God's presence with open hands, naked and vulnerable, proclaiming to ourselves and to others that without God we can do nothing.[16]

We begin our vulnerable mission in prayer for two reasons. First, this is God's mission and God's work. God is the evangelist. 'I planted, Apollos watered, but God gave the growth' (1 Cor 3.6). Being radically reliant on God means being alert to opportunities he gives, the breakthroughs he makes. In the letter to the Colossians Paul urges them to 'Devote yourselves to prayer, keeping alert in it with thanksgiving' (Col 4.2). Being alert, being wakeful, involves a readiness to see where God is at work already, and join in with his activity. As Paul continues, he urges such prayer for himself. 'At the same time pray for us that God will open a door for the word, that we may declare the mystery of Christ' (Col 4.3). Carlo Carretto expresses the meaning of this prayerful dependence on God.

> God can do everything and I can do nothing. But if I offer this nothing in prayer to God, everything becomes possible in me.[17]

But there is another equally important reason why prayer is where we start in vulnerable evangelism. For prayer helps us to define our relationship with God and our standing in God's eyes. 'You have been adopted into the very family circle of God and you can say with a full heart, "Father, my Father"' (Romans 8.14, J B Phillips). Our intimate relationship with God in prayer as God's sons and daughters is the bedrock of our lives and mission. Here we gain the confidence—personally and corporately—to be vulnerable. Our relationship with God, renewed day by day and week by week, by prayer, in the Eucharist, through Scripture, enables us to go out as 'lambs into the midst of wolves' and trust to God the fruits of our mission.

I found this to be true for myself at a time of great vulnerability. The achievements of five years of ministry in this inner-city parish seemed in jeopardy as difficulties arose in relationships at the heart of the church community. A naturally optimistic person, I awoke each morning with a sense of foreboding. I was drawn deeper into prayer and began each day with a conscious affirmation of my relationship with God. 'You are my Father and I am your son. You are my God and I am your child.' That sense of who I was in God helped me face a difficult few months with hope.

Probably the most obvious example of vulnerable evangelism in the final decades of the twentieth century was Mother Teresa and the Sisters of Charity. Their relationship with Jesus, renewed daily at Mass, enables them to see Jesus daily and serve him in the poorest of the poor. Their physical frailty offered in prayer was—and is—the source of a rich work of God across the world.

Priority

Jesus means business. 'Go on your way…Carry no purse, no bag, no sandals' (Luke 10.3, 4a) Jesus' followers are to go as they are, for their work is urgent. 'Greet no one on the road' (Luke 10.4b). This is not a recipe for rudeness but rather another reminder of the urgency of the task. Eastern salutations can be elaborate and time-consuming. This urgency reminds us of the priority of the task. In our missionary situation today we need a clear sense of what are our priorities as the people of God and to stick to them.

In their work on growing healthy churches, Robert Warren and Janet Hodgson have identified that 'A striking characteristic of healthy churches is that they

We need a clear sense of what are our priorities as the people of God and to stick to them

do less than other churches but do what they do to a higher standard.'[18] Offering worship, building community, reaching out in service and witness will be at the heart of any evangelizing community. Sometimes the central tasks of a missionary congregation can be obscured through many other competing demands. Medium-sized or small churches may stretch themselves too far and dilute the effectiveness of their mission. Larger churches may face the same danger through having more resources.

Going to serve a large suburban church I found a community that had become too busy. Finding space in a crowded church programme for a nurture process for enquirers and those wanting to grow in their faith and discipleship was very difficult. The church had a strong rhythm of worship and service, but an inadequate road to faith and discipleship.[19] It took some time to build one and begin to see the work of sharing the gospel grow once more. Churches need a careful examination of priorities if the gospel is to be shared effectively and take root and grow in people's lives.

Partnership
Jesus bids his followers to go in partnership—and look for partners. For some time now there has been a stress in Christian circles in the UK on collaborative models of leadership and ministry, and certainly that is vital in the evangelistic task. 'He sent them on ahead of him in pairs to every town and place where he himself intended to go' (Luke 10.1). This has clear implications for collaborative working with other churches as well as within our own.

It began with the church reaching out in its need and vulnerability

Yet the emphasis on partnership may take us beyond the Christian community. In *The Isaiah Vision* Raymond Fung tells of a church in Central America which inadvertently hit on this aspect of partnership when it faced a crisis over its youth work. The church appealed to the young people themselves and their parents for help, and the result exceeded their expectations. Not only was the youth work saved, but the church for the first time was able to engage significantly with the young people's families, sharing the gospel, seeing some of them start attending worship and come to faith. The outcome was a significant advance for God's mission in that community, but it began with the church reaching out in its need and vulnerability to the young people and their parents and saying, 'Can you help us?'[20]

The first day of my ministry as an inner-city parish priest included a meeting to approve the plans for a new school to replace the dilapidated Victorian buildings of the existing one. But within weeks, the new school had been taken off the Government building programme. A community campaign was born to reverse the decision. The church was committed to the campaign but largely consisted at that time of middle-aged and elderly people who lived outside the neighbourhood. The most vigorous support for the campaign came from the school parent-teacher association, ably led by the headteacher. The alliance of church and PTA and the relationship forged between myself and the headteacher produced a campaign which caught the attention of the media, led to a meeting with the Minister and a year later saw the rebuilding programme restored. But there were other fruits. The school's good reputation in the community began to affect the church, and the close working relationship which the new school campaign had cemented produced co-operation in other spheres—joint services and events and the beginning of a steady flow of new families into the life of the church.

Jesus said, 'Whatever house you enter, first say "Peace to this house!" and if anyone is there who shares in the peace, your peace will rest on that person; but if not, it will return to you. Remain in that house…'(Luke 10.5–7). Jesus encourages his followers to look for the man or woman of peace, and having found them, base their work and ministry from them. Here Jesus is encouraging us to look for partners who are sympathetic (whatever their belief or lack of it) and will open doors for the work of the gospel. In that Central American church the people of peace were the young people and their parents. In that inner-city parish it was the headmaster and the PTA. In *both* situations the church was weak, unable to respond *on its own* to the challenge before it. But as the church recognized that and in its vulnerability sought the help of others in partnership, then the results were greater than just meeting the immediate challenge.

In the situation facing your church—or a church you are seeking to help—who are the partners God is calling you to work with to open doors for the gospel and build up the work of the kingdom?

Presence
'Remain in the same house' (Luke 10.7) said Jesus to his followers. Establish your presence in the neighbourhood and build up relationships there.

As the new school campaign and its successful outcome reverberated in the neighbourhood, so it did in the church as well. Our presence was strengthened. The local church which had sought to serve the community faithfully for more than a hundred years began to grow again and make an impact once more.

Then a new independent church moved into the area, taking over a redundant chapel. At first sight this new church had much more to offer than we had—with more people and more money. When they began a vigorous programme of outreach, I became afraid that our own small shoots of growth might be short-lived. I need not have worried. The new church had no presence in the neighbourhood. It was known as the 'Volvo church.' People came in from all over the city, mostly by car. Their connections with the local community were small, while ours were growing all the time. Partnership had produced trust, relationships were deepening, our presence was being felt, and our hospitality was being matched by others. As we open our hands to others, so they open their hands to us.

The pastoral ministry of the Church of England has always been considered one of its strengths. Smaller numbers of clergy and significant social breakdown in some communities have put this under stress, as has a society where networks are becoming more significant than neighbourhoods in forming relationships. Yet the development of shared ministry teams and the first Anglican network churches have all stressed the need to establish a loving presence as a basis for missionary outreach. If our resources are limited we need prayerful discernment to see where our presence can be most effective.

Practical Service
'Whenever you enter a town and its people welcome you, eat what is set before you, cure the sick who are there and say to them, "The kingdom of God has come near to you"' (Luke 10.8–9). Jesus' followers are to announce the kingdom of God, the reign of God breaking into human life. They are to do so in three ways

- by offering peace
- by healing the sick
- by word of mouth.

The offering of peace for us is like the establishing of a loving presence. The healing of the sick can indeed point to a prayerful concern for the needs of others but will include acts of practical, loving service too. When asked to be part of a pastoral reorganization scheme which suddenly doubled the size of the parish we served, we set up a vigorous visiting campaign, letting people know which their new parish church was. Every home was visited—nearly 2000 houses in all—in a six-month period. It was an enormous effort for a small congregation. The outcome was difficult to assess. There was just one request for ministry.

A few months later a public meeting was called in the new part of the parish to protest at a new road building scheme that would mean the demolition of some homes and a threat to the livelihood of some shopkeepers. I was asked to chair it. After the meeting and others that followed it, when people had seen our practical involvement in their struggles, new opportunities for ministry began to grow. Being good news seemed to go alongside bearing it, and gave integrity to the whole process.

In one of their publications, Springboard asks this question for all churches eager to share the gospel: 'How can we serve the people with whom we already have contact in such a way as to make the gospel intriguing, challenging and appealing?'[21]

Proclamation

Jesus is clear. The message of the kingdom has to be shared in word too. 'Say to them, "The kingdom of God has come near to you"' (Luke 10.9). The witness given in life and action has to be borne in word too. Pope Paul VI drew out the significance of this when he said:

> The finest witness will prove ineffective in the long run if it is not explained, justified—what Peter called always having 'your answer ready for people who ask you the reason for the hope that you all have' [1 Peter 3.15] and made explicit by a clear and unequivocal proclamation of the Lord Jesus. The Good News proclaimed by the witness of life sooner or later has to be proclaimed by the word of life.[22]

But how? Jesus' own way of sharing the gospel of the kingdom was usually through story. As the gospels depict him, his conversation had two main features—he asked questions in order to elicit other people's stories and in response he told his own. Story remains the best way for us too. As John Finney has said, 'Christians have two unique stories to share. The first is the story of Jesus Christ. The second is the story of how we ourselves experience God.'[23] The encouragement of Christians to reflect on and share their stories with each other is a vital tool in encouraging them to do so outside the community of faith.

But is there anyone there to listen? Jesus assumes a long process of personal engagement has taken place before the message is shared. The radical nature of that engagement can easily be missed. The same radical challenge is given in the well-known words at the end of Matthew's gospel when Jesus urges the eleven disciples to

> 'Go therefore and *make disciples* of all nations *baptizing them* in the name of the Father and of the Son and the Holy Spirit and *teaching them* to obey everything that I have commanded you.'
> (Matthew 28.19, 20)

'I don't like those verses!' someone said to me recently at a training day I was running. 'They smack of Christian imperialism!' Certainly these verses have been abused. Medieval European kings used them to stir the passions that led to the Crusades. And there have been other offenders. But properly understood they have much to show us of the nature of Christian proclamation.

First, proclamation arises from *going*. This is a startling emphasis for a religious teacher, who perhaps might have been expected to exhort others to 'Come into the church.' Certainly for Jews, Gentiles were always welcome to learn about Judaism by coming to the synagogue. But to go out and share the message was not part of the religious culture in which the disciples were raised. Moreover for those so challenged, the cost was clear. It is much easier, more comfortable and less threatening to meet people on our own territory than to join them on theirs.

Secondly, they speak of the important work of *nurturing* people in the Christian faith—through a process of exploration and explanation which needs to be tailored to the enquirers' needs and concerns and able to help them grow in understanding.

Thirdly, these verses speak of baptism as not just the doorway to the community of faith but a crucial step of a *life-long journey* of teaching, development and growth. The goal is mature discipleship, 'to the measure of the full stature of Christ' (Eph 4.13).

St Matthew points up the words of Jesus as his last will and testament by making them the completion of his gospel. He records too that they were met initially by an uncertain response. 'When they saw him, they worshipped him, but some doubted' (Matt 28.17). As John Drane has commented:

> There is not much sign of imperialistic self-confidence here. This is not the militaristic clarion call of 'Onward Christian soldiers marching as to war.' On the contrary, Matthew depicts a group of people whose starting point is their own weakness—people with at least as much doubt as faith, who were prepared to go out into other people's territory not to conquer it but with an overwhelming sense of their own inadequacy and vulnerability.[24]

Then as now Jesus' followers are sent out: 'Go on your way. See, I am sending you out like lambs among wolves' (Luke 10.3). We go as a vulnerable community in the name of the one whose wounds bring us healing and whose love has so won our hearts that we commit ourselves to a task whose outcome is uncertain and whose cost is great—but go we must!

> Churches are free to choose the ways they consider best to announce the gospel to different people in different circumstances. But these options are never neutral. Every methodology illustrates or betrays the gospel we announce. In all communications of the gospel, power must be subordinate to love.[25]

Questions for Reflection

- Looking at the life of your own church—or a church you are seeking to serve—which of the six characteristics of the evangelizing community (from Luke 10) are the strongest and the weakest? Why?
- In what sense does your church 'go' to seek to share the gospel?
- What does this chapter say to you personally?

Vulnerable Evangelism in Practice 5

The Curate and the Couple

A curate began to visit a young couple in his parish who were expecting their first child. The curate was conscientious in his pastoral care, but the couple, fairly typical young professionals, were friendly enough but without much interest in what he had to offer as a Christian priest.

The child was born, but soon became seriously ill and died. The curate was deeply upset by this and visited the couple to bring some comfort to them. To his distress he was unable to say anything, but just sat in the living room crying. He left feeling a complete failure as a priest.

To his astonishment the couple came to church the following Sunday. 'I don't understand it,' he said. 'When you needed me most I had nothing to give you.' The couple replied, 'But you gave us everything you had.' The curate had shown that he was one with them in their loss. His wordless communication had revealed to them Christ's self-giving love.[26]

At the School Gates

On Wednesday 13 March 1996 Dunblane became a household name all over the world. That day the normally quiet Scottish rural city was changed forever by the brutal murder of 16 young children and their teacher, victims of a crazed gunman. For the whole community and many more beyond Dunblane and Scotland it was one of those defining moments when ultimate questions about the meaning of life and death took on a new significance.

Two days later, Dunblane's ancient cathedral was crowded, as thousands of people sought a place of quietness and spiritual consolation in the midst of their grief. During that day John Drane has described how

> I must personally have prayed with literally hundreds of people ... They were not for the most part regular Church attenders, and it was a new experience for me to walk down the street and be accosted by complete strangers who just wanted to be held in silence and assured of God's presence with them in their shock and sorrow.[27]

At the end of the day John Drane needed some space for himself to reflect. He made his way to the school gates which had become a centre of devotion. Now, the only people there were a gang of youths aged about 17–20.

As he watched, the young people took from their pockets 16 small candles and one large one—one for each dead child and for their teacher. Kneeling on the pavement, they arranged them in a circle and carefully lit them from their cigarettes. They stood quietly for a moment, until one of them said, 'I suppose somebody should say something.'

As they wondered how to do that, they caught sight of John Drane, identified him as a minister and called him over. 'You'll know what to say.' The reality was very different. As he stood there, with tears streaming down his face, he had no idea what to say or how to say it. As John Drane explains,

> Words had not been especially useful to me, or anyone else in this crisis. So we stood, holding onto one another for a moment, and then eventually I spoke. I have no recollection of what I said. It certainly was not a formal 'churchy' kind of prayer, but it provided the cata-

lyst that enabled them to start praying. A question came first: 'What kind of world is this?' another asked, 'Is there any hope?' Someone said, 'I wish I could trust God.' 'I'll need to change,' said a fourth one. As he did so, he looked first at me, and then glanced over his shoulder to the police who were on duty. He reached into his pocket and I could see he had a knife. He knelt again by the ring of candles and quietly said 'I'll not be needing this now,' as he tucked it away under some of the flowers laying nearby. One of the others produced what looked like a piece of cycle chain, and did the same. We stood silently for a moment, and then went our separate ways.[28]

John Drane saw that the young people were

...meeting with God in a profound way. Though they would not have used this language they were repenting. They were reaching out. They were searching for a better way of living—for God's kingdom.[29]

At the Crossroads

In November 1995 Yorkshire Water threatened to cut off the water supply to Meltham on alternate days because of the drought. A group of Christians arranged a meeting to discuss how the church could help elderly people caught without water.

During the meeting someone said, 'I keep looking at the empty shop on the corner and wondering if the churches could use it.' Everyone else there had had the same thought. Enquiries were made and three months later the 'Crossroads' project was set up to serve the needs of the local community. In February 1996 the Crossroads shop opened, selling second hand clothes and household goods, with all the profits going to the community.

Now there is a Crossroads Centre as well, funded by the shop, with various agencies involved. The Centre aims to provide a safe and welcoming place for people seeking help to find acceptance, information and advice.

The project was born of prayer and continues to be a venture of faith. As Jean Burhouse, Secretary of the Project has said

As we prayed for the new venture things seemed to fall into place. So many people were very enthusiastic and wanted to be involved. We didn't encounter any major problems and we were very encouraged. We have drawn inspiration from Christ's feeding of the 5,000. God has taken the little we have offered and made much from it.

Some £800 a week is currently raised for local community needs and community based projects in other parts of the world.

As Crossroads has served the community, it has sought to bear 'a positive Christian witness.' That is shown by the spirit of mutuality at the heart of the project. The many volunteers who run the shop and assist in the Centre speak of receiving as much as they give. Those who receive also give in return and it has been noticeable how this giving and receiving has reached right across the community.

Many lives have been touched. A young mother in her first day in Meltham seeking refuge from a difficult domestic situation, found friendly help and practical support through Crossroads. As many people in Meltham say, 'This is the best thing to have happened in Meltham.'

In the Supermarket

In April 1999 Damian Feeney and his family moved to Longsands, Preston. A new housing area developed in the 1990's, Longsands had no church building. Damian had been appointed as mission priest for Longsands—but where would the customary licensing service be held?

Fiona, Damian's wife, suggested the ASDA supermarket. It was the main meeting place in the neighbourhood. The deputy manager agreed and such was the publicity generated, that Damian was able to hold a weekly Eucharist from the licensing in June 1999.

It was celebrated on Sunday at 10am in the concourse of the supermarket next to the Cafeteria, where people were eating their breakfast. Orders of service were placed on each Cafeteria table. The service lasted half an hour including an address and prayers of intercession and Damian wore full vestments.

People were queuing around the service to get into the store which technically opened at 10.30. There was a small regular congregation, although as many as 150 people encountered the service in some way. Afterwards the congregation put the tables away and had breakfast together. Then Damian visited the store and was available to staff. He also visited regularly one afternoon during the week and much pastoral ministry has developed.

The initial ASDA congregation has formed the nucleus of another congregation which has been planted in the Millennium Hall, a new community hall nearby. This meets on Saturday evening and attracts 20–30 people with a children's liturgy of the word as well as a full eucharistic liturgy. The ASDA Communion service existed principally as a place of outreach and availability, an opportunity for chance encounter—both with neighbour and with the living God.

Damian Feeney comments from his Anglican Catholic perspective:

> I firmly believe that one of the failures of Catholicism in recent years
> has been to try to protect Christ's presence. The celebration of the
> Eucharist at ASDA has taught me above all how very robust God is. I
> have learned again and again how ready Christ is to sit with sinners
> and the apathetic in much the same way as he did during his earthly
> life. Of course there are days when the apathy is upsetting—but the
> one who submitted himself to the nails of the cross does not require
> protection from Sunday shoppers.[30]

Conclusion 6

Vulnerable evangelism takes its inspiration from Jesus. It seeks to share the
gospel in Jesus' way. It seeks to live out the cross in daily life.

George Macleod, the founder of the Iona Community, wrote in 1956:

> I simply argue that the cross be raised again at the centre of the mar-
> ket-place as well as on the steeple of the church. I am recovering the
> claim that Jesus was not crucified in a cathedral between two can-
> dles, but on a cross between two thieves; on the town garbage heap;
> at a crossroad so cosmopolitan that they had to write his title in He-
> brew and in Latin and in Greek; at the kind of place where cynics talk
> smut, and thieves curse, and soldiers gamble. Because that is where
> he died. And that is what he died about. And that is where church-
> men should be and what churchmanship should be about.[31]

For both evangelists and the church, the way of vulnerable evangelism is the
way of honest and open reliance upon God and deep solidarity with our
fellow humans. For only in that solidarity can we truly commend the gospel—as D T Niles famously said—as 'one beggar showing another beggar
where to find bread.'[32]

Notes

1   *Good News People* (Church House Publishing, 1999) p 48.

2   *ibid*, p 48.

3   From a taped interview on *Evangelism Today* published by York Courses.

4   Richard Giles, *We do not Presume* (Canterbury Press, 1998) p 57.

5   The Whole Story Christian Festival, Leeds 1976.

6   Mission England, Sheffield 1985.

7   Last verse of the poem 'Jesus of the Scars' by James Shillito, quoted in William Temple, *Readings in St John's Gospel* (Macmillan, 1968) p 366.

8   John Drane, *Faith in a Changing Culture* (Marshall Pickering, 1997) pp 134–135.

9   Jurgen Moltmann, *The Open Church* (SCM) p 108.

10   Vanessa Heyrich and Ivan Mann have maintained that vulnerability lies at the heart of the very meaning of the incarnation and therefore has far-reaching implications for all Christian ministry and leadership. See Heyrich and Mann, *Jesus Wept* (Darton, Longman and Todd, 1998) and especially pp 9–16.

11   Pope Paul VI, *Evangelization in the Modern World* (CTS Publications, 1976) p 7.

12   Russ Parker, *Free to Fail* (SPCK, 1992) p 73.

13   A view the Jews based on Genesis 10 where there are seventy names in the Hebrew text and seventy-two in the Septuagint (the Greek version of the Old Testament).

14   John R H Moorman, *The Path to Glory* (SPCK, 1961) p 121.

15   Quoted by Clifford Longley, *The Tablet*, 2 December 1995.

16   *Seeds of Hope: A Henri Nouwen Reader* (DLT, 1998) p 65.

17   Carlo Carletto, *Letters from the Desert* (DLT, 1972) p 136.

18   *Growing Healthy Churches*, a resource produced by the Missionary Congregations Project Team, a joint venture of Springboard and the Board of Mission, p 4.

19   The images of the rhythm and the road are taken from Steven Croft, *Ministry in Three Dimensions* (DLT, 1999) pp 158–159.

20   Raymond Fung, *The Isaiah Vision* (Geneva: WCC, 1992) pp 36–37.

21   *Preparing for Mission Weekends* from Springboard, 4 Old Station Yard, Abingdon, Oxon, OX14 3LD.

22   Pope Paul VI, *op cit*, p 12.

23   John Finney, *Finding Faith Today* (Bible Society, 1992) p viii.

24   John Drane, *Faith in a Changing Culture*, p 73.

25   *Mission and Evangelism—An Ecumenical Affirmation* (WCC, 1982) section 28.

26   David Day tells this story in *A Preaching Workbook* (SPCK, 1998) p 61.

27   John Drane, *Faith in a Changing Culture*, p 29.

28   *Faith in a Changing Culture*, p 30.

29   *ibid*, p 30.

30   For a fuller reflection on the ASDA service see George Lings, *Encounters on the Edge No.16* (Church Army, 2002).

31   George Macleod, *Only One Way Left* (The Iona Community, 1956) p 38.

32   Quoted by John Young, *Teach Yourself Christianity* (Hodder and Stoughton, 2003) p 196.